When Daddy Goes on Storm

Krista Conway

DEDICATION

For linemen and their families who
sacrifice so much to maintain our way of life.

And to my lineman who has given so much of himself for others.

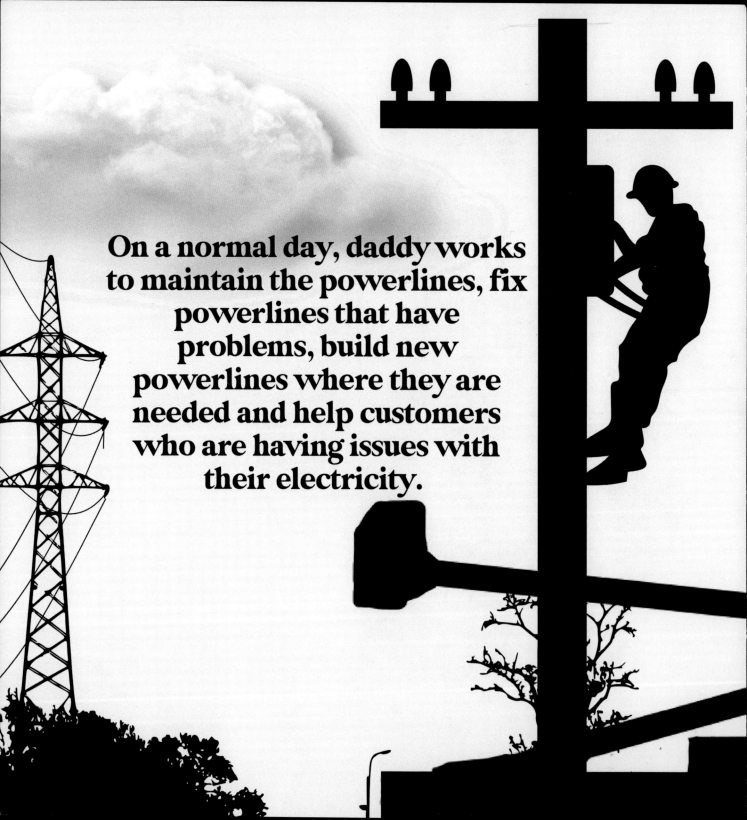

On a normal day, daddy works to maintain the powerlines, fix powerlines that have problems, build new powerlines where they are needed and help customers who are having issues with their electricity.

Sometimes weather or natural disasters damage all of the powerlines in large areas. When this happens, it takes hundreds or even thousands of linemen to repair the damage and restore power to the people who were effected.

When Daddy goes on storm, he packs a storm bag with all of the clothes he will need. Sometimes he takes food, water and a pillow.

Even though I might not see him for a while, I know Daddy will come home when he is done getting the power back on to the people who need it.

Hurricanes

Hurricanes bring high winds, heavy rain and other weather events all at once. When a hurricane hits land, damage to homes and the power grid can range from minimal to devastating.

The amount of damage done by a hurricane depends on where and how they come ashore and what category they are when they make landfall. Sometimes they cause minimal damage, other times they can completely destroy the entire power grid. This means Daddy and his co-workers might have to start over with the entire power system.

With hurricanes, Daddy might be gone a few days or even several weeks.

Wind Storms

Wind storms can pop up out of nowhere with very little notice. They can effect a small area or many states all at once.

Wind speed impacts the amount of damage done during a wind storm. If an area has a lot of trees that fall on powerlines, it can take even longer to restore power.

Just like with hurricanes, it can take days or even weeks to repair the damage done by wind storms.

Wild Fires

Wildfires can burn hundreds or even thousands of acres at a time. Everything in a wildfires path is burnt, including poles and powerlines.

Wild fires completely destroy the power system where they burn. Most of the time they have to be completely rebuilt.

It can take weeks to repair the damage.

Ice & Snow Storms

Ice and snow storms can bring down powerlines because the build up on the lines is so heavy. Additionally, trees covered in ice and heavy snow can buckle under the weight and fall on lines.

It is common for large areas to have several long lines of poles and towers buckle under the weight of snow and ice.

This means repairing or replacing miles of line. It can take many days or even a few weeks to repair ice and snow storm damage.

Earthquakes

Earthquakes shake the earth. Sometimes earthquakes are hardly felt. Other times Earthquakes can do extensive damage. The shaking felt during an earthquake can cause poles to fall over.

Just like with hurricanes, earthquakes have a rating system. The bigger the number on the magnitude scale, the more damage they cause. Earthquakes that cause a lot of damage are rare.

Tornadoes

Tornadoes create high winds in a small area. They often pop up unexpectedly and can go for miles. Powerlines are broken or even pulled out of the ground.

Most of the time tornadoes cause damage to a small area. Typically the damage is contained and can be repaired quickly by a team of linemen. Like hurricanes and earthquakes, tornadoes also have a rating system that tells us how strong they were.

Daddy might be gone a few days up to a few weeks, depending on the F-Scale rating the tornadoes were given and where they occurred.

Mudslides

Mudslides typically happen after a heavy rain causes the earth to give way. The heavy mud and rocks can break power poles and bury them under mud.

Daddy will have to wait for excavators to make the land safe before he can repair damage to mud slide areas.

He might be gone a few days to repair the damage.

Floods

Floods can occur after a heavy rainfall, dam breaks or during other weather events, like hurricanes.

Floods can cause poles to pop out of the ground or break under the pressure of the water.

It can take days or weeks for Daddy to finish repairs after a flood.

When Daddy goes out to work a storm, the people he is helping have endured a major weather event, followed by the loss of power. Helping people get their power back means they can turn their lights on, keep food cold in their refrigerator, take a warm bath and so much more.

When it's over, Daddy comes home.

He is a hero.

The End

we hope you loved this book.

Krista married her lineman in 2000 and together they have four linekids.

Krista has created an information page on her website for kids to learn more about storms. She has also created printable worksheets and more to go along with this book.

Find more books and the details about the information mentioned above at

www.KristaConway.com/books

Made in the USA
Las Vegas, NV
19 December 2024

14943754R00017